P9-CEC-987

AN INSIDE LOOK

EXPLORING THE
OCEANS

For a free color catalog describing Gareth Stevens Publishing's list of high-quality books and multimedia programs, call 1-800-542-2595 (USA) or 1-800-461-9120 (Canada). Gareth Stevens Publishing's Fax: (414) 332-3567.

The editors would like to extend thanks to Keith A. Sverdrup, Associate Professor, Department of Geosciences, University of Wisconsin-Milwaukee, Milwaukee, Wisconsin, for his kind and professional help with the information in this book.

Library of Congress Cataloging-in-Publication Data available upon request from publisher. Fax: (414) 332-3567 for the attention of the Publishing Records Department.

ISBN 0-8368-2726-0

This North American edition first published in 2000 by
Gareth Stevens Publishing
A World Almanac Education Group Company
330 West Olive Street, Suite 100
Milwaukee, WI 53212 USA

This U.S. edition © 2000 by Gareth Stevens, Inc. Original edition © 1998 by Horus Editions Limited. First published as *Exploring the Oceans* in the series *How It Works* by Horus Editions Limited, 1st Floor, 27 Longford Street, London NW1 3DZ, United Kingdom. Additional end matter © 2000 by Gareth Stevens, Inc.

Illustrators: Jim Channell, David Hardy, Sebastian Quigley, Steve Seymour, Steve Weston, and Gerald Witcomb
Gareth Stevens editors: Christy Steele and Heidi Sjostrom

Printed in Mexico

3 1559 00126 9594

1 2 3 4 5 6 7 8 9 04 03 02 01 00

AN INSIDE LOOK

EXPLORING THE

OCEANS

Stephen Hall

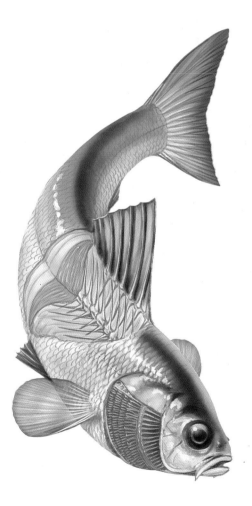

Gareth Stevens Publishing
A WORLD ALMANAC EDUCATION GROUP COMPANY

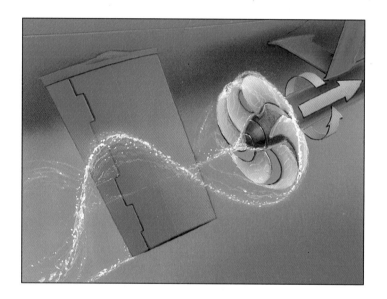

AN INSIDE LOOK

CONTENTS

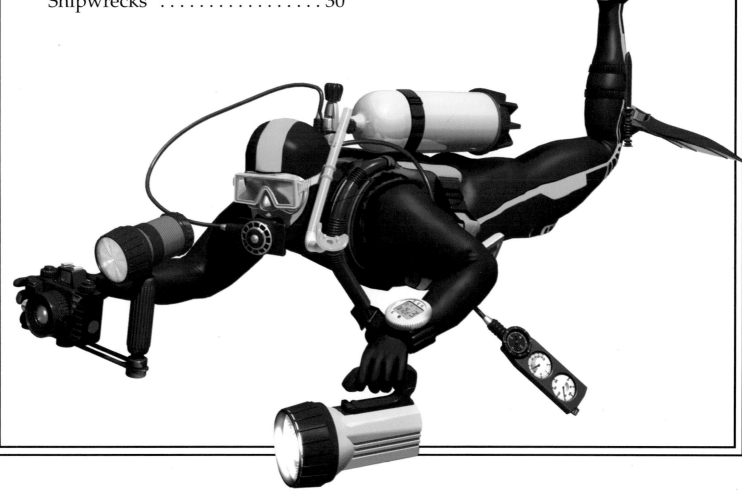

The Ocean Floor

The ocean floor covers 71 percent of Earth. Like dry land, the ocean floor has many different features. Tall mountains, trenches, valleys, and flat plains also lie deep under the ocean.

The ocean floor is part of Earth's crust. The crust layer of our planet rests on top of the mantle, the rocky middle layer. The crust and the upper part of the mantle are broken into huge pieces called plates. The plates drift slowly over melted mantle rock.

The ocean floor lies on plates made of oceanic rock. This rock is only about 1/3 mile to 3 miles (.5 to 5 kilometers) thick. New oceanic rock forms at spreading ridges where plates are moving away from each other. Rock is destroyed in subduction zones. At this point, gravity pulls rock down into the mantle, where it melts.

Water fills the ocean basins. The amount of liquid water available on Earth varies with Earth's ice ages. Today, water covers the continents' lower edges. These submerged parts are called continental shelves.

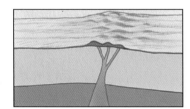

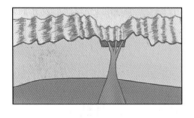

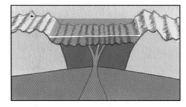

The birth of an ocean
Volcanic activity starts along a weak point in Earth's crust (*left, top*). The crust cracks when two or more plates move away from each other. This forms a steep-sided valley like the Great Rift Valley in Africa (*left, middle*). The valley may flood and, over millions of years, widen into an ocean (*left, bottom*). Long ago, the African and American plates split. The Atlantic Ocean filled the gap.

AS MOUNTAINS ARE WORN DOWN BY THE WEATHER, RIVERS CARRY ROCKS AND SOIL INTO THE OCEAN.

THE OCEAN FLOODS LOW-LYING LAND WHEN SEA LEVELS RISE.

THE EDGES OF A CONTINENT SLOPE DOWNWARD TO MEET THE DEEP OCEAN FLOOR.

⑤

MOLTEN ROCK RISES AND THEN HARDENS TO FORM THE CORE OF MOUNTAINS.

OCEANIC CRUST SOMETIMES CONTINUES BELOW THE THICKER CONTINENTAL CRUST.

NEIGHBORING ISLANDS USUALLY SHARE THE SAME CONTINENTAL SHELF.

MAJOR RIVERS CAN CARVE VALLEYS INTO THE CONTINENTAL SHELF WHEN SEA LEVELS ARE LOW.

THE DEEP OCEAN FLOOR IS CALLED THE ABYSSAL PLAIN.

MID-OCEAN RIDGES FORM THE LONGEST MOUNTAIN CHAINS ON EARTH.

Moving plates

In some places, the edges of two plates rub past each other and form faults, such as the San Andreas fault in California. Sometimes plates crash into each other to produce mountain ranges, such as the Himalayas. Some plates move away from each other, as they do in the mid-Atlantic Ocean. Over millions of years, continents and oceans completely change position. Britain has sometimes been covered by ocean waters and was once as far south as the state of Florida is now.

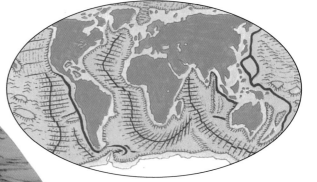

MANY ISLANDS ARE REALLY THE TOPS OF LARGE VOLCANOES THAT ARE RISING FROM THE OCEAN FLOOR.

A CORAL REEF CAN FORM AROUND THE RIM OF AN ERODED (WORN-DOWN) VOLCANIC ISLAND.

THE OCEAN FLOOR IS MADE UP OF LAYERS OF ROCK AND SEDIMENT. SEDIMENT IS MUD, CLAY, AND SAND.

MAGMA (MOLTEN ROCK) FROM THE MANTLE RISES AND FLOWS THROUGH CRACKS IN THE SPREADING RIDGES.

VOLCANOES FORM IN PLACES WHERE MAGMA SQUEEZES THROUGH THE OVERLYING CRUST.

Seafloor features

The ocean floor spreads apart at a ridge (see left, 1). Magma rises from beneath the crust and hardens to form new oceanic rock. Except for seamounts (2), most of the abyssal plain (3) is flat and covered in a thick layer of fine-grained sediment called ooze. The tops of flat-topped seamounts (4) were worn down by waves. These hills sank beneath the ocean's surface as they moved away from ridges. Underwater landslides leave piles of sediment (5).

7

Tides

Each day, the ocean's water level rises and falls periodically. This regular change in the water level is called a tide. Earth's ocean waters are pulled into an oval shape around the planet. The Moon circles Earth in a path called an orbit. As the Moon orbits Earth, its gravity affects the ocean's level. The Moon's pull makes waters rise on the side of Earth closest to the Moon and creates a tidal bulge, causing a high tide. The spinning of Earth and the Moon also makes a tidal bulge on Earth's opposite side.

The tidal range is the difference between high-water and low-water levels. In some seas, the tidal range is only about 1 inch (2.5 centimeters). The Bay of Fundy in Canada has the world's largest tidal range at 50 feet (15 meters). The largest tidal ranges occur where a shallow or narrow coastline strengthens the tidal effects. Tidal ranges change with surges caused by storms, wind direction, the presence of islands or other land, and tidal friction against the seafloor.

The effects of the Sun and Moon

In the diagram below, you can see how the oceans bulge outward toward the gravitational pull of the Moon and the Sun (effects are exaggerated here to make them clearer). When the Moon and Sun are in line, their gravitational pulls together create a large spring tide (*2 and 4*). The greatest tides occur during the spring and autumn equinoxes when the Sun is directly over the equator and is lined up with the Moon. When the Moon and Sun are not lined up to pull in one direction, (*1 and 3*), the Moon's effect on the oceans is stronger than the Sun's. However, the Sun pulls from a different direction, so it neutralizes the Moon's pull, and the tidal bulges are smaller. A small neap tide occurs. Many plants and animals have learned to use tidal ranges.

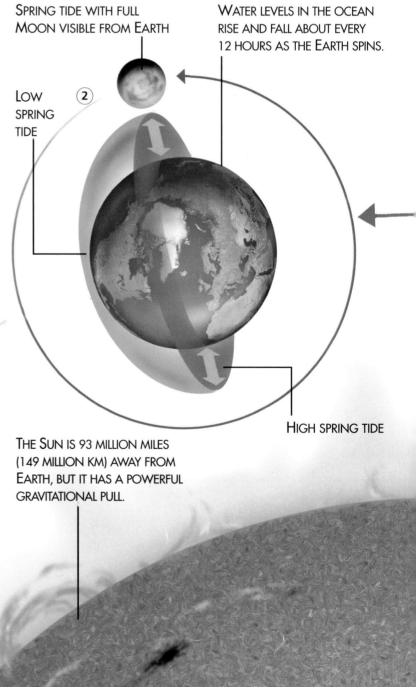

SPRING TIDE WITH FULL MOON VISIBLE FROM EARTH

WATER LEVELS IN THE OCEAN RISE AND FALL ABOUT EVERY 12 HOURS AS THE EARTH SPINS.

LOW SPRING TIDE

②

HIGH SPRING TIDE

THE SUN IS 93 MILLION MILES (149 MILLION KM) AWAY FROM EARTH, BUT IT HAS A POWERFUL GRAVITATIONAL PULL.

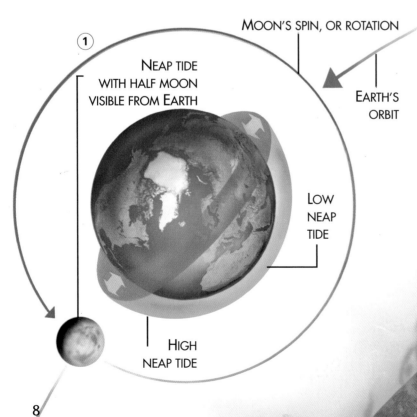

MOON'S SPIN, OR ROTATION

①

NEAP TIDE WITH HALF MOON VISIBLE FROM EARTH

EARTH'S ORBIT

LOW NEAP TIDE

HIGH NEAP TIDE

LOW NEAP TIDE   LOW SPRING TIDE   HIGH NEAP TIDE   HIGH SPRING TIDE

Tidal range and plant growth

Because of the regular rise and fall of the oceans, plants and animals live at particular heights along the shoreline. Only salt-resistant lichens live in the splash zone. To stay alive, green seaweeds and barnacles need to be low enough to be covered by water at high tide.

Tidal ranges

The positions of the boat and views of the Moon show the differences between spring and neap tides.

When the Moon is full or new, we get spring tides with large tidal ranges. At half moon, the tidal difference is much smaller.

NEAP TIDE WITH HALF MOON VISIBLE FROM EARTH.

③

LICHENS LIVE IN THE SPLASH ZONE, WHICH IS ABOVE THE HIGH-TIDE MARK.

HIGH-TIDE WATERS REACH GREEN SEAWEEDS, LIMPETS, AND BARNACLES.

BROWN SEAWEEDS LIVE NEAR THE LOW-TIDE MARK, SO THEY ARE UNDERWATER MOST OF THE TIME.

RED SEAWEEDS OFTEN GROW BELOW THE LOW-TIDE MARK.

SPRING TIDE WITH CRESCENT, OR NEW MOON, VISIBLE FROM EARTH.

THE TIDAL RANGE IS LARGE WHEN THE SUN AND MOON PULL FROM THE SAME DIRECTION.

④

THE TIDAL RANGE IS SMALL WHEN THE SUN AND MOON ARE AT RIGHT ANGLES.

Waves and Wind

About fifty different currents flow through Earth's oceans. Several start at the equator, where the Sun shines directly overhead. The strong sunlight heats the ocean waters. As the water gets warmer, it moves out toward the North and South poles. At the icy poles, the water becomes cooler and flows back toward the equator. Then the cycle begins again. This is how currents of water move deep in the oceans. Surface currents are caused by blowing winds, the spin of Earth, and the position of nearby landmasses.

Winds also cause waves as they blow over the surface of the sea. The water itself does not move forward in a wave on the open sea. The water particles merely go around in a circle. Only the energy that this movement makes will move forward.

The Beaufort Scale

The Beaufort Scale, developed in 1808, is used at sea to describe the wind's strength. This system relies on signs that people can see rather than on scientific instruments, but it is still a valuable warning of stormy seas.

0 calm, sea like a mirror
1 light air, small ripples
2 light breeze, small wavelets
3 gentle breeze, wave crests begin to break
4 moderate breeze, small waves and some "whitecaps"
5 fresh breeze, larger, moderate waves, many whitecaps
6 strong breeze, large waves 10 feet (3 m), foam crests and spray
7 near gale, rough seas, blowing spray or foam
8 gale, waves up to 20 feet (6 m) high
9 strong gale, tumbling waves up to 30 feet (9 m) high
10 storm, white ocean surface, visibility is difficult, waves up to 40 feet (12 m)
11 violent storm, sea covered in foam, small ships lost to view between wave crests
12 hurricane, waves more than 45 feet (14 m) high; spray fills the air.

STRONG WINDS CAUSE WHITECAPS.

WAVES OVER 60 FEET (18 M) ARE RARE, BUT ONE WAVE OF 112 FEET (34 M) WAS RECORDED IN 1933.

A SHIP IN GOOD CONDITION SAILED BY A SKILLED CREW CAN WITHSTAND THE MOST VIOLENT STORMS.

IN A FORCE-11 STORM, FOAM COVERS THE SEA.

THE EYE OF THE STORM

COOL, DESCENDING AIR

WARM, ASCENDING AIR

THUNDERCLOUDS

WALLS OF DENSE CLOUD

WINDS OF MORE THAN
75 MILES (120 KM) PER HOUR
GUST BELOW THE STORM.

AIR SPIRALS IN TOWARD
THE EYE OF THE STORM.

Great storms

Tropical revolving
storms called typhoons,
hurricanes, or cyclones
form over warm water and
can reach over 300 miles
(480 km) in diameter.
Wind speeds are 75 miles
(120 km) to 155 miles
(250 km) per hour or
more. Warm, moist air is
sucked into the storm and
begins a counterclockwise
spiral upward. Walls of
dense cloud form rings
around the storm's center,
or eye. The eye is a calmer
area of cool, falling air.
These storms cause serious
damage if they pass over
land, but they die out as
they move inland away
from the coast.

LIGHT BREEZES CAUSE
SMALL WAVELETS.

AT THE END OF EACH WAVE,
WATER PARTICLES ARE BACK
WHERE THEY STARTED.

AS WAVE HEIGHT INCREASES,
THE ANGLE OF THE CREST
GROWS STEEPER.

IN A FORCE-8 GALE,
WAVES RISE UP TO
20 FEET (6 M) HIGH.

DEEP BELOW A WAVE, THE
CIRCULAR MOTION OF THE
WATER PARTICLES IS SMALLER.

Surface waters

The colors on the
map below show the
temperatures of land
and ocean surface waters.
The temperatures were
measured by a satellite
as it orbited Earth.
Warm equatorial
temperatures are shown
in orange. Cool polar
temperatures are colored
green and blue.
    The arrows on the
map show where surface
currents flow. Warm

currents are in red; cold
currents are in blue. The
spin of Earth swings these
wind-driven currents to
one side. This creates large
circular currents in the
oceans. Currents flowing
at different depths
connect all of the oceans.
The currents affect the
climate. For example,
warm waters from the
Gulf of Mexico enter the
Atlantic Ocean and move
north, helping to keep
northern Europe warm.

THE WATER PARTICLES
IN THE WAVE MOVE IN A
CIRCULAR PATTERN. ONLY
THE ENERGY OF THE WAVE
MOVES FORWARD.

THE EQUATOR IS THE
IMAGINARY LINE AROUND
EARTH'S MIDDLE, HALFWAY
BETWEEN THE NORTH AND
SOUTH POLES.

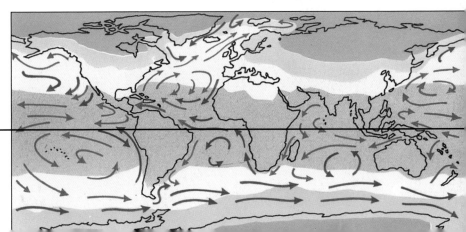

Coastlines

Ocean waters are constantly changing and wearing down coastlines. Coastal land made of hard, volcanic rock survives the pounding of storm waves best. Soft sandstone, on the other hand, is easily worn away. The ocean will also flow through large cracks called faults, or break apart any weak rocks. How steeply coastal rocks slope into the ocean also affects a coastline's shape.

Coasts are popular places for people to live, work, and take vacations. Engineers try to save rapidly eroding coastlines by building sea defenses, such as walls of concrete or stone. Beaches are sometimes preserved with walls or jetties called groins. In some countries, whole areas of low-lying land have been reclaimed from the sea by building walls called dikes and then pumping away the seawater.

Large rivers help save coastlines. As they enter the sea, rivers deposit many tons of mud, stone, and sand onto the seafloor, which builds up natural sea defenses.

Speed of erosion

How long a coastline will last is determined by several factors, such as the hardness of the rock, the fierceness of the sea, and the presence of sea defenses. If rocks under a coastline sink, the sea will flood an area that was once dry land.

Over thousands of years, sea levels change. This also affects how coastlines are eroded. For example, during the last ice age, areas of land were covered in ice. Eventually, the ice melted and released water back into the sea. Also, since the weight of the ice was not pressing on the land, it slowly rose up again. This explains why many places have ancient beaches high above the present sea level.

COVES ARE FORMED WHEN THE SEA OPENS A GAP THROUGH A NECK OF HARD ROCK AND FLOWS INTO SOFTER ROCK BEHIND.

LIKE THE SEA, A RIVER WILL FLOW THROUGH ROCK WEAKENED BY A GEOLOGICAL FAULT.

SAND DUNES FORM IN SHELTERED AREAS.

ABANDONED HOUSES SLIDE DOWN A RAPIDLY ERODING CLIFF.

DEBRIS WILL SOON BE WORN DOWN INTO SAND BY WAVES.

Coastal waves

Waves become shorter and steeper as they approach the coast. This is because the circular motion of water particles within the wave gets pushed upward by the sloping seafloor. The wave breaks once it has reached its maximum steepness. The water then sweeps back out to sea as backwash.

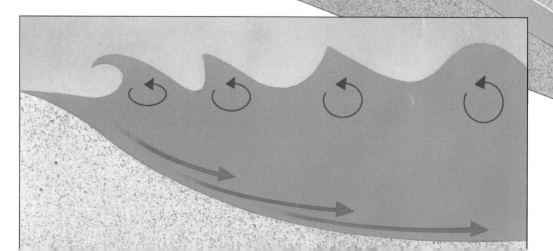

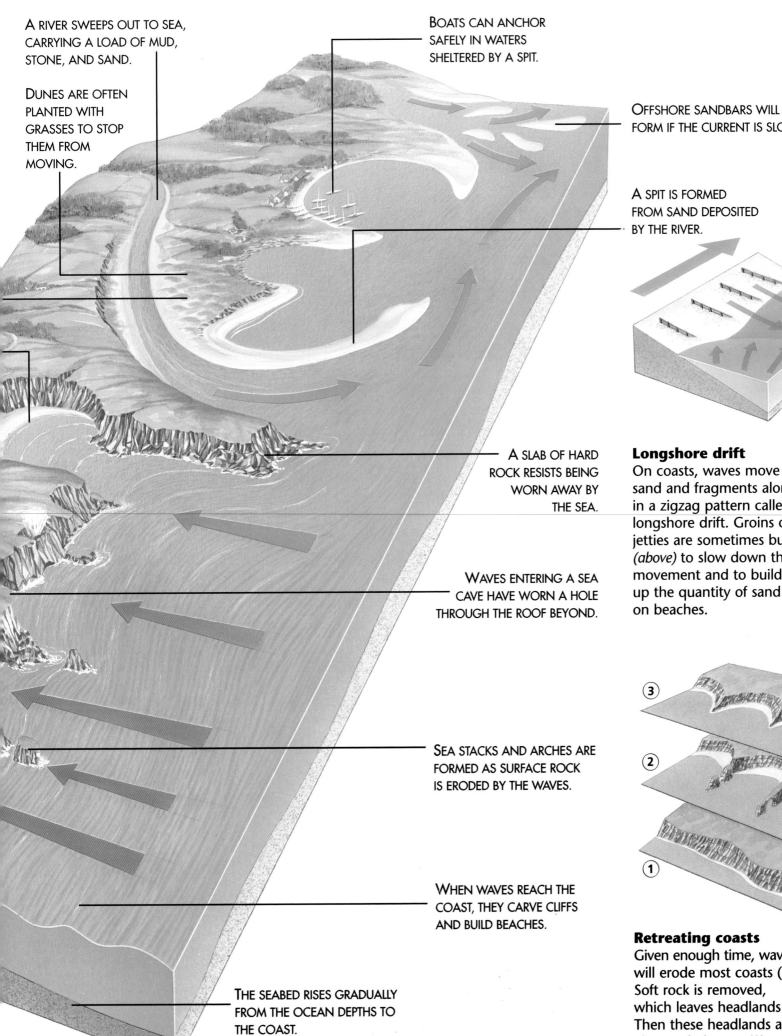

A RIVER SWEEPS OUT TO SEA, CARRYING A LOAD OF MUD, STONE, AND SAND.

DUNES ARE OFTEN PLANTED WITH GRASSES TO STOP THEM FROM MOVING.

BOATS CAN ANCHOR SAFELY IN WATERS SHELTERED BY A SPIT.

OFFSHORE SANDBARS WILL FORM IF THE CURRENT IS SLOW.

A SPIT IS FORMED FROM SAND DEPOSITED BY THE RIVER.

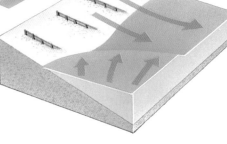

A SLAB OF HARD ROCK RESISTS BEING WORN AWAY BY THE SEA.

WAVES ENTERING A SEA CAVE HAVE WORN A HOLE THROUGH THE ROOF BEYOND.

SEA STACKS AND ARCHES ARE FORMED AS SURFACE ROCK IS ERODED BY THE WAVES.

WHEN WAVES REACH THE COAST, THEY CARVE CLIFFS AND BUILD BEACHES.

THE SEABED RISES GRADUALLY FROM THE OCEAN DEPTHS TO THE COAST.

Longshore drift

On coasts, waves move sand and fragments along in a zigzag pattern called longshore drift. Groins or jetties are sometimes built (*above*) to slow down this movement and to build up the quantity of sand on beaches.

Retreating coasts

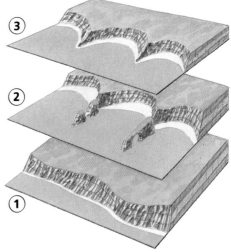

Given enough time, waves will erode most coasts (1). Soft rock is removed, which leaves headlands (2). Then these headlands are also eroded away (3).

Frozen Seas

The extreme northern and southern regions of our planet are very cold. The Arctic, in the north, is an ice-covered ocean, surrounded by Greenland and the northern continents. Antarctica, in the south, is a huge continent surrounded by the Southern, or Antarctic, Ocean.

Many huge masses of slowly moving ice called glaciers have joined to form the ice caps that cover much of Greenland and Antarctica. Cold winds freeze other parts of the sea, while warm winds and currents can occasionally melt some sea ice (*right*).

Few creatures live on the surface of the frozen seas, but a rich variety of fish and plankton lives near the edges of the ice. Larger animals, such as seals and whales, eat this food.

Melting ice

The amount of ice on Earth changes over time. For example, 25,000 years ago, glaciers covered most of the northern hemisphere. So much water was frozen as ice that the sea level was much lower than it is now.

But, if Earth's temperature rose and all of the ice that rests on land melted, the sea level would be much higher than it is now because extra water would be added to the oceans. The extra water would flood beaches and cities on low coastal lands.

RISING WARM WATER MELTS AN AREA OF ICE.

ICEBERGS FROM ICE CAPS CAN BE LARGE ENOUGH TO SERVE AS AN AIRCRAFT LANDING.

RIDGES OF ICE FORM WHERE SHEETS OF PACK ICE BUMP INTO EACH OTHER.

THE SEA BEGINS TO FREEZE, FORMING PANCAKE ICE. THESE SHEETS GRADUALLY JOIN EACH OTHER TO FORM PACK ICE, OR AN ICE FLOE.

AN ICEBREAKER BATTERS ITS WAY INTO THE PACK ICE.

AT THE BOUNDARY WITH WARMER WATER, THE ICE EDGE BECOMES THINNER AND GRADUALLY DISAPPEARS.

SEASONAL FALLING OF COLD WATER AND RISING OF WARM WATER BRINGS NUTRIENTS TO FEED TINY PLANTS AND ANIMALS CALLED PLANKTON.

FOR SIX MONTHS OF THE YEAR, THE SUN DOES NOT SHINE IN FAR NORTHERN OR SOUTHERN REGIONS.

OVER MANY YEARS, GLACIERS BUILT UP TO FORM THE VAST ANTARCTIC ICE CAP.

THE WEIGHT OF A POLAR ICE CAP PULLS IT DOWNHILL. IT IS FORMED FROM SNOW AND ICE THAT HAVE BUILT UP OVER THE CENTURIES.

FREEZING WINDS BLOW OUT TO SEA FROM THE ICE-COVERED LAND.

ICE SHEETS CAN EXTEND OUT TO SEA FOR SEVERAL MILES (KM).

WHEN SEAWATER FREEZES, SALT IS LEFT BEHIND. THE SALTY WATER SINKS, WHICH STARTS WATER CIRCULATION.

GIANT LUMPS OF ICE CALLED ICEBERGS BREAK AWAY FROM THE ICE EDGE IN A PROCESS CALLED CALVING. THEN THE ICEBERGS DRIFT OUT TO SEA.

WARM, LESS SALTY WATER FLOWS UP TOWARD THE SURFACE, WHERE IT WILL COOL AND FREEZE, CONTINUING THE CYCLE.

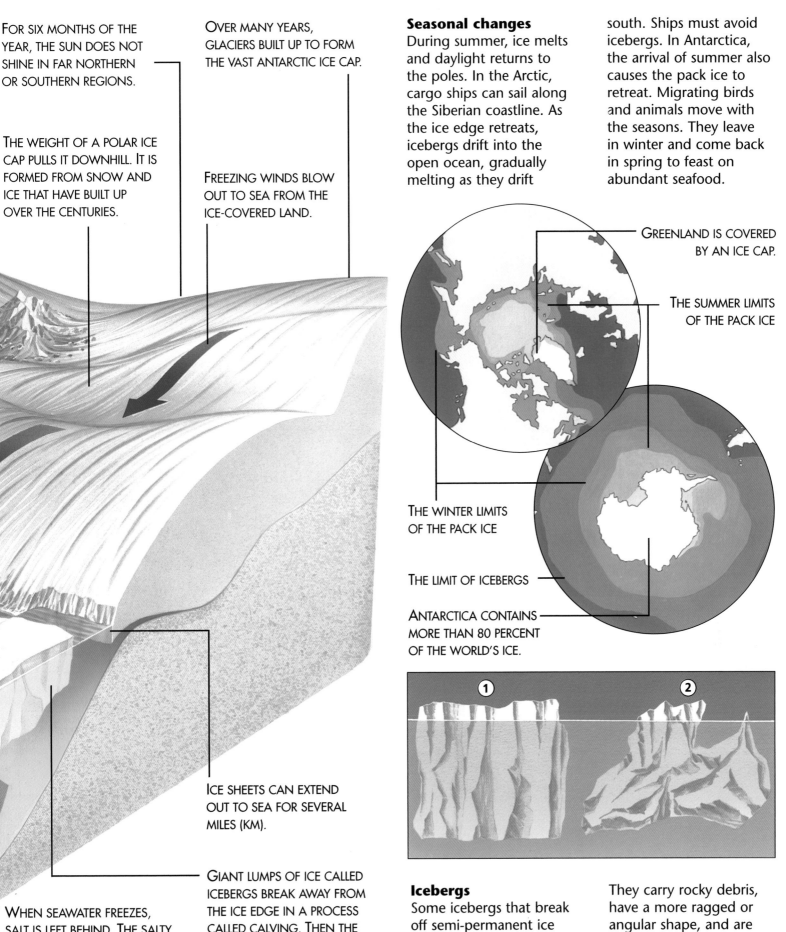

Seasonal changes

During summer, ice melts and daylight returns to the poles. In the Arctic, cargo ships can sail along the Siberian coastline. As the ice edge retreats, icebergs drift into the open ocean, gradually melting as they drift south. Ships must avoid icebergs. In Antarctica, the arrival of summer also causes the pack ice to retreat. Migrating birds and animals move with the seasons. They leave in winter and come back in spring to feast on abundant seafood.

GREENLAND IS COVERED BY AN ICE CAP.

THE SUMMER LIMITS OF THE PACK ICE

THE WINTER LIMITS OF THE PACK ICE

THE LIMIT OF ICEBERGS

ANTARCTICA CONTAINS MORE THAN 80 PERCENT OF THE WORLD'S ICE.

Icebergs

Some icebergs that break off semi-permanent ice caps are as large as an island and take months or even years to melt (1). They have table-like, flat tops, so they are called tabular. Icebergs that break off glaciers are much smaller in size (2). They carry rocky debris, have a more ragged or angular shape, and are mostly found in the Arctic, which is the area near the North Pole.

Nine-tenths of an iceberg is underneath the water. As it melts, it may become unstable and capsize.

15

Mapping the Sea

Oceanographers are scientists who use special tools to study the oceans and the animals and plants that live in them. They use an instrument called a sonar (*so*und *na*vigation and *r*anging) to measure the depth of the ocean and to make pictures of what the ocean floor looks like. Sonar sends sound waves through the water, and it records data when the sound bounces back off objects on the ocean floor. Scientists use coring devices to pull up columns of earth that show what soils make up the ocean floor. They lower or tow devices from research ships to measure the temperature, saltiness, and chemistry of the ocean. They also analyze water samples in laboratories. Satellites measure sea surface temperature, winds, wave heights, and even plankton cover. Subsurface drifters and pilotless submarines roam the depths, reporting findings with radio or cable connections.

SPECIAL RADAR EQUIPMENT CAN LOOK THROUGH CLOUDS TO RESEARCH THE OCEAN BELOW.

WAVE HEIGHTS CAN BE MEASURED BY SATELLITE ALTIMETERS, WHICH ARE VERY ACCURATE EVEN FROM A HEIGHT OF 830 MILES (1,334 KM).

A BATHYSONDE RECORDS THE OCEAN'S TEMPERATURE, SALINITY (SALT CONTENT), AND PRESSURE.

THE GIANT PISTON CORER IS USED FOR REMOVING LONG, DEEP SAMPLES OF OCEAN FLOOR.

Towed instruments
A planelike, undulating vehicle is towed behind a research ship. It travels deep down from the surface and then travels back up, all the time gathering data, such as water temperature. A side-scan sonar is also towed. It gathers data to map the shape of the seabed.

16

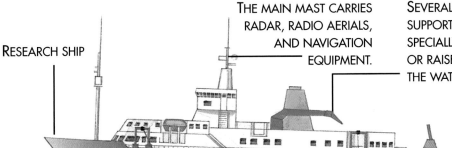

RESEARCH SHIP

THE MAIN MAST CARRIES RADAR, RADIO AERIALS, AND NAVIGATION EQUIPMENT.

SEVERAL CRANES AND SUPPORTING FRAMES ARE SPECIALLY MADE TO LOWER OR RAISE EQUIPMENT FROM THE WATER.

WATER BOTTLES ARE FILLED AT SELECTED DEPTHS TO TEST THE SALTINESS.

Research ships

Research ships carry scientists and technicians who sail for several weeks at a time to gather information about the ocean. Because these ships are very expensive to run, there are only a few of them. Robot explorers, like the ROV (remote operated vehicle) shown left (1), are being developed to collect data when ships are not available or to go on dangerous missions, such as exploring under ice caps. Scientists leave behind moored buoys (2) to measure ocean currents and temperature. The buoys emit radio signals, so the scientists can retrieve them.

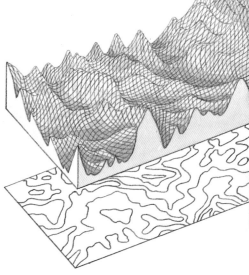

What lives at the bottom?

More than 6,600 feet (2,012 m) down in the North Atlantic Ocean, giant marine isopods swim along the ocean floor. Special time-lapse cameras take pictures of deep-sea animals.

Charts and maps

Computers help produce maps of the seafloor by turning sonar images into three-dimensional pictures. Engineers use the maps to plan where to lay cables and pipelines or how to safely navigate submarines.

Plankton recorder

This device is towed behind ships to measure how much plankton lives near the sea surface. Plankton are microscopic. Seawater and plankton enter through the front, and a fine silk mesh inside catches the plankton. The plankton is then stored in a cylinder to be analyzed later at a laboratory.

Grab sampler

As its name implies, the grab sampler scoops a sample of the ocean floor and brings it up.

Computer models

Information about the ocean is fed into special computer programs called models, which can show how the ocean works. Models can help predict the route of accidental oil spills or how the ocean will respond to climate change.

Early Ships

Until the invention of steam power, sailors had to use sails or oars to move their ships forward. For hundreds of years, explorers used wind power to travel all over the oceans.

All of the earliest ships relied on oars and wind. The Vikings and Polynesians rowed for days if the wind was not behind them, and ancient Greeks and Romans forced slaves to row their warships and trading ships. It took many centuries for people to learn how to build ships that could move without having to rely on the wind to push them.

Only in the last one hundred and fifty years did sails finally give way to other forms of propulsion. In the nineteenth century, steam power began to replace sails, and people constructed steel ships instead of wooden ships. In the early twentieth century, oil began to replace coal as fuel. Steam-piston engines were followed by steam turbines. Some military vessels still use steam turbines and have nuclear reactors to make the steam.

Developments since steam

Ships such as the *Titanic* were built to carry people and mail across oceans quickly. After World War II (1939–1945), aircraft took over that role, so large passenger ships were used as cruise liners instead. Steamships are being retired because newer diesel engines are less expensive to run. In the 1970s, people began to build faster gas turbine (jet engine) ships, but they burn a lot of fuel. Today, the good acceleration and speed of gas turbines that recirculate exhaust heat benefit military ships.

Ancient ships

Egyptians made long-distance voyages in boats built of reeds, palm fiber, and tar. Modern copies of these boats have crossed the Atlantic and northern Indian oceans. Other early ships were built of animal skins and wood. Many of these boats were used to cross open oceans, though we do not know how many boats sank while trying.

AN EGYPTIAN REED BOAT FROM AROUND 2,000 B.C.

IN 1843, THE *SS GREAT BRITAIN* WAS THE FIRST OCEAN-GOING SHIP TO BE BUILT OF IRON. IT WAS THE FIRST PROPELLER-DRIVEN STEAMSHIP TO CROSS THE ATLANTIC.

THE CROW'S NEST IS WHERE LOOK-OUTS WATCHED FOR ICEBERGS.

A TOTAL OF 1,503 PEOPLE DIED WHEN *TITANIC* SANK ON APRIL 14, 1912.

TITANIC HAD TWO OUTBOARD RECIPROCATING STEAM ENGINES AND ONE STEAM TURBINE ENGINE.

THE *MAYFLOWER* CARRIED
PILGRIM SETTLERS TO THE NEW
WORLD (AMERICA) IN 1620.

THE *MAYFLOWER* WAS TINY
AND TOOK 65 DAYS
TO CROSS THE
ATLANTIC.

From sail to steam

Few changes were made to
sailing ships until about the
fifteenth century, when the
Americas began to attract
voyagers from the other
side of the Atlantic. By the
nineteenth century, the
sailing ship was perfected.

At the same time, however,
the invention of steam
power made it possible
for ships to travel in any
direction without depend-
ing on the wind. Some
journeys that had taken
months to complete only
took a few weeks.

THREE FUNNELS WERE REAL;
ONE WAS ONLY AN AIR VENT.

TITANIC HAD THREE
PROPELLERS AND
ONE HUGE RUDDER.

TITANIC DID NOT
CARRY ENOUGH
LIFEBOATS FOR
EVERYONE; NOW
THE LAW MAKES
SURE SHIPS DO.

LENIN WAS A RUSSIAN
ICEBREAKER AND THE
FIRST SURFACE SHIP TO BE
FUELED BY NUCLEAR POWER.

Nuclear power at sea

Only a small number of
nuclear-powered civilian
(non-military) ships have
been built. The Russians
chose nuclear power for
their large ice-breaking
ships because the ships
could clear the sea lanes
off their northern coasts
without having to
constantly return to
base for refueling.

THREE NUCLEAR REACTORS
GAVE A MAXIMUM SPEED
OF 18 KNOTS.

LENIN COULD CLEAR A
CHANNEL 90.5 FEET (27.5 M)
WIDE THROUGH PACK
ICE 8 FEET (2 M) THICK.

19

Modern Ships

Running ships cheaply is now more important than traveling at top speed. Most modern ships are built of steel and powered by diesel engines. They are usually equipped with automated machinery so that only a small crew is needed. Satellites and computers control navigation with traditional instruments, such as the sextant, available for backup.

Speed is still important to some specialist ships, such as express ferries, which commonly use twin-hull designs. These catamaran designs allow ships to travel at high speeds without using a lot of expensive fuel. In the future, there will be more ships using two or three small, streamlined hulls. Their narrow, smooth shapes cut more easily through water. Any water resistance can slow a ship down, so ships with streamlined shapes go faster.

Luxury cruise liner
People traveling quickly between places no longer choose ocean liners. Now, people take their vacations on board ocean liners. Instead of high speed, the main goal has become comfort, so ships have smooth-running diesel engines, stabilizers to steady the ship and prevent rocking, and air conditioning for comfort.

Why do ships float?
A ship's metal hull encloses a lot of air and displaces, or pushes aside, a lot of water. One cubic foot or cubic meter of ship weighs far less than one cubic foot or cubic meter of water, so a ship floats. A solid metal ship would sink.

THE FUNNEL, OR STACK, CARRIES AIR IN AND EXHAUST OUT FOR THE MAIN ENGINES.

INDOOR AND OUTDOOR SWIMMING POOLS ARE FOUND ON BOARD.

SATELLITE COMMUNICATIONS EQUIPMENT PROVIDES CONSTANT CONTACT WITH THE MAINLAND.

EXERCISE ROOMS, SHOPPING MALLS, AND HAIRDRESSERS ARE ALL AVAILABLE ON BOARD.

PASSENGERS RELAX ON THE AFT DECK.

ROPES CAN BE USED TO HELP THE SHIP DOCK.

TWIN RUDDERS STEER THE SHIP. CROSSWINDS CAN EASILY BLOW SUCH A HIGH-SIDED SHIP OFF COURSE.

LIFEBOATS AND RAFTS ARE ABOARD, SO PASSENGERS CAN ESCAPE IN EMERGENCIES.

Stabilizers

Most passenger ships use winglike stabilizer fins to reduce rocking and keep the ships steady (see opposite, top). Stabilizers use gyroscopes, computer software, and hydraulic jacks to react quickly to the ship's roll and provide lift or down-force, so the ship is kept on an even keel. When the sea is calm, stabilizers are pulled inside the ship to prevent damage.

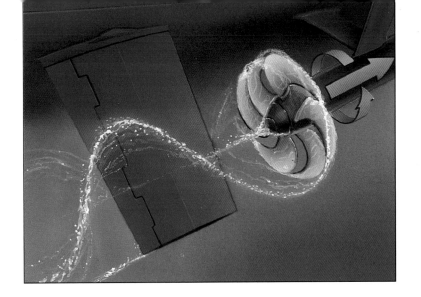

Propeller design

Great care goes into the design and manufacture of propellers. If just one blade is out of balance, the smooth propulsion of a ship can be ruined. Modern designs use several curved blades. On some ships, the blades can be rotated for reverse thrust to move back.

THE MOST EXPENSIVE CABINS ARE HIGHER UP ON THE SHIP.

THE BRIDGE HOUSES THE SHIP'S MAIN CONTROLS.

THE FORWARD WEATHER DECK CAN WITHSTAND HEAVY WAVES.

NAVIGATION, RADIO, AND RADAR EQUIPMENT ARE CARRIED ON THE MAIN MAST.

THE FORWARD AUDITORIUM IS A FULL-SIZE THEATER.

A BOW THRUSTER HELPS THE SHIP TURN.

STABILIZER FINS ENSURE A COMFORTABLE CRUISE.

HEAVY EQUIPMENT, FUEL, AND SUPPLIES IN THE LOWEST PART OF THE SHIP AID STABILITY.

ELECTRIC MOTORS TURN THE PROPELLER SHAFTS.

POWERFUL DIESEL ENGINES TURN GENERATORS TO PROVIDE ELECTRICITY FOR ALL THE SHIP'S NEEDS.

Satellite navigation

Global Positioning System (GPS) satellites carry highly accurate atomic clocks and send time and position data to GPS receivers that are fitted to ships and aircraft. The satellites measure latitude, longitude, altitude, and speed. The receiver compares signals from two or more satellites and can work out a ship's position to within a few feet (m). Buoys with radio beacons also help confirm a ship's position near those points.

Fishing

Many people around the world enjoy eating seafood. Because the demand for fish and squid is so high, there are always large fleets of fishing vessels on Earth's oceans. To stop people from catching too many fish, nations check on and control fishing within 200 international nautical miles of their coasts. Governments use aircraft or satellites to search for illegal fishing activity. The inspectors can go aboard fishing vessels to be sure regulations are being followed.

A fishing crew lives and works aboard ship twenty-four hours a day. They are often paid according to the value of the catch. Even today, deep-sea fishing is a physically tiring and dangerous job.

Factory ship
Fishing grounds can be a long way from the country where the fish will be eaten. Some ships are equipped like factories, so they can turn fish into products that can be sold at the voyage's end, which might be several months away. On board, the fish are gutted, and the quality fish fillets are sorted and frozen. The fish organs are stored or processed into oils and chemicals, and the heads, bones, and other parts that were cut off are turned into fish meal, pastes, and cheaper foods. Nothing is wasted. The ship will stay at sea until the hold is full of fish or until fuel runs low.

THE A-FRAME KEEPS THE NET AND CABLES FROM GETTING CAUGHT ON THE SHIP'S STERN.

COMPUTER-CONTROLLED WINCHES (REELS) KEEP THE NET AT THE RIGHT DEPTH.

AS THE CATCH ARRIVES, THE CREW SETS TO WORK CLEANING AND PROCESSING THE FISH.

CREW MEMBERS CAN HARNESS THEMSELVES TO RAILS, SO THAT THEY ARE NOT SWEPT OVERBOARD IN ROUGH SEAS.

CRANES ARE USED TO HANDLE THE CABLES AND NETS.

THE NET IS HAULED BACK ON BOARD USING THE SLOPING STERN RAMP.

A POWERFUL PROPELLER AND DOUBLE-HINGED RUDDER MAKE THE SHIP EASIER TO STEER AND MANEUVER.

THE ENGINE ROOM PROVIDES POWER FOR WINCHES AND THE SHIP'S ELECTRICAL SUPPLY.

THE MAIN DIESEL ENGINE IS HEAVY AND SITS DEEP IN THE HULL, WHICH HELPS STABILITY.

ABOVE THE BRIDGE IS A FULL SET OF NAVIGATION, COMMUNICATION, AND RADAR AERIALS.

ACCURATE NAVIGATION EQUIPMENT KEEPS THE VESSEL WITHIN THE LEGAL BOUNDARIES FOR FISHING.

ALL OF THE VESSEL'S OPERATIONS CAN BE CONTROLLED FROM THE BRIDGE.

LIGHTS ON THE FOREMAST WARN OTHER SHIPS TO STAY CLEAR OF THE NETS.

THE FOREDECK HAS LIFEBOATS, ANCHOR CHAINS, THE FOREMAST, AND CAPSTANS FOR WRAPPING THE HUGE PULLING ROPES.

Sonar on fishing boats

Sonar has several functions on fishing boats. By reflecting off the seabed, it measures the water's depth and shows where fish are. Trawlers use sonar to track the net's position and depth. Otterboards that hold the net open are fitted with sonar to detect how wide the mouth of the net is. A sonar at the net's end alerts the boat when the net is full.

CREW MEMBERS SLEEP IN BUNKS. THEY WORK VERY HARD BOTH NIGHT AND DAY.

PROCESSED FISH IS DEEP-FROZEN IN THE HOLD.

THE STRONG STEEL HULL ALLOWS THE BOAT TO OPERATE IN ICY WATERS.

NETS HAVE DIFFERENT MESH SIZES THAT ALLOW YOUNG FISH TO ESCAPE.

Fishing methods

Some fish and squid are caught using bright lights (1). The lights attract them to the water's surface at night so they can be caught on baited hooks. Drift nets (2) can be several miles (km) long. Trawl nets (3) are towed at a set depth by a fishing boat and hauled in when they are full. A purse-seine net (4) surrounds an entire shoal or group of fish, and then scoops them all up from the water.

DRIFT NETS CAN BE DANGEROUS, TRAPPING DOLPHINS, TURTLES, AND BIRDS. THEY ARE BANNED FROM EUROPEAN WATERS.

Submarines

Many submarines are currently operating in Earth's oceans. A few are small, carrying just two or three passengers. People use them to conduct scientific research or construction work. Small submarines are called submersibles because they can stay underwater for only a few hours at a time.

Military submarines are much larger. Some of them can stay underwater for several months. To dive beneath the water's surface, the crew allows seawater to flood the submarine's large ballast tanks. Also, propellers on the back of the ship speed the ship downward at an angle determined by the horizontal rudders, which are flat instead of straight up and down. The diesel-electric submarine is the quietest type of sub. It is used for missions where underwater silence is important.

Staying hidden
The most important challenge for military submarines is to avoid being found, so they rarely surface, raise periscopes, or use radios. Because sound carries easily underwater, submarines are built to be as quiet as possible. Mechanics are taught to be careful not to drop their tools, and, if necessary, the submarine will sit motionless for days. The inertial guidance systems in current submarines navigate using gyroscopes to sense the ship's movements. Surfacing to look through a periscope is not necessary using these guidance systems.

Nuclear submarines
Nuclear submarines are powered by an on-board nuclear reactor. The reactor creates steam that is used to turn the ship's propellers and to generate the electricity needed to live on and operate the ship. Air and water for the crew and for operating machinery are also manufactured on board. Because it can take a year or more for the nuclear fuel to be used up, these ships can stay at sea for very long voyages. Sailors for these ships must be able to handle the small, crowded spaces of a submarine and be willing to be away from home for long periods.

THE NAVIGATION BRIDGE IS USED WHEN THE SUBMARINE HAS SURFACED.

FORWARD FINS CAN BE RAISED VERTICALLY TO HELP THE SUBMARINE SURFACE THROUGH ICE.

THE UPPER SURFACES ARE STRENGTHENED TO COPE WITH SURFACING THROUGH ICE.

EMERGENCY ESCAPE HATCH

BALLAST TANKS

THE STREAMLINED NOSE AIDS SPEED AND REDUCES NOISE.

INSIDE THE NOSE IS THE SONAR DOME, WHICH EMITS SOUNDS TO DETECT OTHER SOLID OBJECTS IN THE SEA.

LAUNCH TUBE

A COVERING OF SOFT TILES ABSORBS SOUND.

BUNKS FOR THE CREW MUST FIT INTO ANY AVAILABLE SPACE.

THE HULL IS MADE FROM STEEL, TITANIUM, OR CERAMIC MATERIALS AND IS STRONG ENOUGH TO DIVE MORE THAN 1,969 FEET (600 M).

Detection by sound

A submarine uses sonar to detect solid objects. Sonar can be active (the submarine emits sounds that are reflected back from an object) or passive (the submarine just listens to the noises that other vessels or large animals are making).

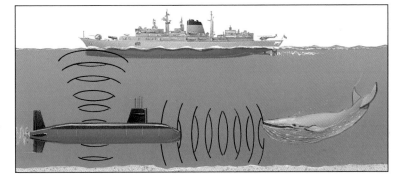

A MISSILE IS LAUNCHED FROM THE TUBE WITH A PUFF OF GAS. ITS ROCKET ENGINE LIGHTS AS IT REACHES THE WATER'S SURFACE.

A NUCLEAR REACTOR CAN OPERATE FOR SEVERAL YEARS WITHOUT REFUELING.

LARGE RUDDERS KEEP THE SUBMARINE STEADY.

THE PROPELLER IS DESIGNED TO MAKE LITTLE NOISE AND NO BUBBLES.

THE CONNING TOWER CARRIES THE RADAR, PERISCOPES, AND COMMUNICATION EQUIPMENT.

A LOT OF THE SUBMARINE'S SPACE IS TAKEN UP BY ITS CARGO.

HATCHES

BALLAST TANKS

STEAM IS GENERATED AS WATER PASSES THROUGH THE REACTOR, AND IT DRIVES A TURBINE.

THE TURBINE GENERATES ELECTRICITY FOR THE MAIN MOTOR AND ALL THE SUBMARINE'S SYSTEMS.

MISSILES HAVE SOLID-FUEL ROCKET ENGINES.

Diving and surfacing

In order to sink, a submarine has to become heavier. It does this by filling large ballast tanks with seawater (1). If it has to surface, compressed air is blown back into the ballast tanks

to push out the water (2). This makes the submarine lighter again and more buoyant and able to float. Some submarines have been lost at sea when something has gone wrong with the ballast tank system.

EMERGENCY BATTERIES HELP IF THE MAIN POWER FAILS.

MISSILES ARE CARRIED IN TUBES. THEY CAN BE LAUNCHED WHILE THE SUBMARINE IS UNDERWATER.

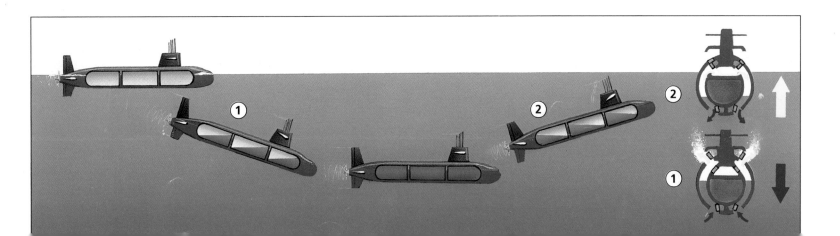

Scuba Diving

Scuba (*s*elf-*c*ontained *u*nderwater *b*reathing *a*pparatus) allows people to explore the underwater world. With scuba equipment, divers can breathe special air mixtures and swim underwater to a depth of about 130 feet (40 m), sometimes to 328 feet (100 m). At greater depths, the water pressure has dangerous effects on divers, and their thinking could be clouded.

Pioneers like Jacques Cousteau and Hans Hass made scuba diving very popular. Today, people dive all around the world. In fact, diving has become a problem in some places. Too many divers can damage fragile corals and affect the normal behavior of fish.

Although diving is quite safe, training is essential. Divers learn safety skills and calculate how long they have been down, so they can surface without getting the bends, a painful condition that develops when air bubbles form inside the body.

Breathing apparatus
The tank strapped to the diver's back contains air for the diver to breathe. At the top of the air tank, level with the diver's lungs, is a valve called a regulator. Air passes through the regulator and down a tube to the mouthpiece. The regulator reduces the pressure of the air that comes out of the tank. The pressure is also reduced by the demand valve in the mouthpiece. This ensures the air

THE REGULATOR CONTROLS THE FLOW OF AIR FROM THE AIR TANK AND REDUCES THE AIR'S PRESSURE.

AIR PIPES TO THE MOUTHPIECE

THE FACE MASK ENABLES THE DIVER TO SEE UNDERWATER.

FLASH UNIT FOR CAMERA

ELECTRICAL ITEMS MUST BE WATERPROOF.

UNDERWATER PHOTOGRAPHY IS OF GREAT INTEREST TO MANY SPORT DIVERS.

DEMAND VALVE

A DIAPHRAGM IN THE VALVE EQUALIZES AIR AND WATER PRESSURE.

DIVER BREATHES IN THROUGH A VALVE.

AIR TUBE TO THE BC JACKET

FLOW OF EXHAUST AIR FROM BREATHING OUT

divers breathe is at the same pressure as the water around them. Divers must not hold their breath but at all times breathe smoothly because air expands as they travel up to the surface, and it could burst their lungs!

THE AIR TANK CARRIES HIGHLY COMPRESSED, OR CONCENTRATED, AIR MIXTURES.

DIVERS MUST TAKE CARE NOT TO DAMAGE CORALS WITH THEIR FINS.

SWIM FINS ARE USED TO PROPEL THE DIVER.

NEOPRENE WET SUIT, HAT, GLOVES, AND SOCKS KEEP THE COLD OUT.

DIVERS CARRY A KNIFE TO USE IF THEY GET TANGLED IN NETS, LINES, OR SEAWEEDS.

THE WET SUIT'S BRIGHT COLORS MAKE THE DIVER EASIER TO SEE.

A BUOYANCY COMPENSATOR (BC) IS A JACKET THAT CAN BE INFLATED WITH AIR TO HELP THE DIVER RISE TO THE SURFACE.

A WEIGHT BELT HELPS THE DIVER SINK EASILY.

A COMPASS AND GAUGES SHOW DIVE DEPTH AND THE AMOUNT OF AIR LEFT IN THE TANK.

THE COMPASS IS ESSENTIAL IN MURKY WATERS.

MANY DIVERS USE A DIVE COMPUTER TO KEEP TRACK OF TIME AND TO CALCULATE THE SPEED AT WHICH THEY ARE RISING TO THE SURFACE.

"OK." – EVERYTHING IS ALL RIGHT ON THE SURFACE.

"NOT OK." – HELP NEEDED ON THE SURFACE.

"ARE YOU OK?" – "I AM OK."

"HELP!"

Wet suits

In a wet suit, a layer of neoprene foam rubber insulates the diver against cold. Divers buy wet suits with different thicknesses of foam, depending on the water temperature. A wet suit is designed so that water leaks into it through the neck, leg, and armholes. The body then warms up the thin layer of water between the wet suit and skin, keeping the diver warm for hours.

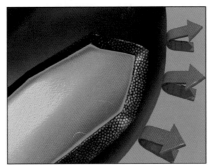

Hand signals

Although there are gadgets that enable you to speak underwater, most divers do not have them, so they rely on hand signals. There is an international code of hand signals so that divers can work safely anywhere in the world. Divers never dive alone. They always have a fellow diver to keep an eye on them and watch for distress signals.

Submersibles

Submersibles are small, deep-diving vehicles that were first used to search for wreckage of lost aircraft, ships, and weapons. Today, they are most often used by scientists exploring mysterious features of the deep ocean floor, such as trenches and volcanic ridges. Compared with military submarines, submersibles cannot stay under the surface of the water for very long, usually only a few hours, or a day or two at the most. However, they can dive much deeper than any military submarine, some to 19,686 feet (6,000 m) or more. They also have windows, camera systems, and mechanical hands, so the crew can view and handle objects at the bottom of the sea.

Today, rigid diving suits can do almost the same job as submersibles. Some armored suits, such as the *Newt* suit, use small propellers to push the suit through the water.

Trieste 1

Trieste 1 was designed to reach the greatest depths possible. On January 23, 1960, it carried Jacques Piccard and Lt. Don Walsh to the record depth of 35,840 feet (10,924 m) at the bottom of the Pacific Ocean's Mariana Trench.

Trieste had two ballast tanks filled with heavy iron pebbles. To surface, the iron pebbles were released, making *Trieste* lighter and able to rise. A large tank filled with gasoline gave buoyancy. The crew sat in a steel sphere below the tanks.

A LARGE TANK, CALLED THE FLOAT, PROVIDED BUOYANCY.

THE UNDERWATER TELEPHONE TRANSMITTER IS USED TO CALL PEOPLE ON THE SURFACE.

THE TOWER IS BRIGHTLY COLORED SO THAT IT CAN EASILY BE SEEN WHEN THE CRAFT HAS SURFACED.

THE SONAR SCANNER CAN FIND HIDDEN OBSTACLES.

TELEVISION CAMERAS RECORD EVERYTHING HAPPENING OUTSIDE. PLENTY OF LIGHTS PENETRATE THE DARKNESS.

THE CABIN IS LIKE A METAL BALL.

MECHANICAL ARMS COLLECT OBJECTS FROM THE OCEAN FLOOR.

WITH THE HELP OF LASER TECHNOLOGY, ARM CONTROL IS PRECISE.

TWO TANKS CONTAINED METAL BALLAST.

A COLLECTING CAGE CARRIES SAMPLE BOTTLES, ROCK SPECIMENS, AND ITEMS FROM SHIPWRECKS.

BALLAST TANKS HOLD
SEAWATER AND AIR.

SIDE THRUSTERS CONTROL
UP-AND-DOWN MOVEMENT.

SEVERAL THRUSTERS PROPEL
AND STEER THE CRAFT.

THE OUTSIDE HULL IS MADE
OF COMPOSITE MATERIALS.

Rigid diving suit

A rigid (armored) diving
suit resists water pressure
at depths of more than
2,625 feet (800 m). The
pressure inside the suit
remains the same as it is at
the surface, enabling the
diver to work comfortably
inside it. The whole suit
weighs just 48 pounds
(22 kilograms) underwater
and is flexible enough
for the diver to walk up
ladders, roll on the seabed,
and get up again.

ELECTRIC CONTROLS ARE
KEPT IN PROTECTIVE TANKS.

BATTERIES PROVIDE
POWER TO RUN
THE MOTORS
AND ELECTRICAL
EQUIPMENT.

THIS TANK CONTAINS AIR
FOR THE CREW TO BREATHE.

PORTHOLE

A STRONG TITANIUM FRAME
AND LANDING SKIDS PROTECT
THE VESSEL UNDERWATER.

IRON WEIGHTS CAN BE
RELEASED IN AN EMERGENCY
TO MAKE THE CRAFT RISE.

DIFFERENT TOOLS CAN BE
FITTED TO THE HANDS.

THE *NEWT* SUIT IS MADE
OF METAL, GLASS FIBER,
AND CERAMICS.

Alvin

Alvin has been used since
1964 to explore the
ocean floor. After many
modifications, it can
now reach a depth of
14,765 feet (4,500 m).
Alvin gained fame in
1966 when it found a
lost nuclear bomb, which
was then safely recovered.
In the 1970s, *Alvin* took
the first pictures of deep-
sea volcanic vents, which
are hot-water springs
that are rich in oceanic
chemicals (*see page 32*).
In 1986, *Alvin* explored
the wreck of the *Titanic*
(*see page 18*).

29

Shipwrecks

In an average year, about 150 ships sink due to accidents, severe storms, and, most commonly, human error. Some of these wrecks cause major pollution problems, such as oil spills. However, the ocean's natural forces are able to cope with most types of waste. Iron-eating bacteria start consuming the ship's hull, worms eat up the wood, and chemical action breaks down what is left. After a few hundred years, natural processes have destroyed much of the shipwreck, leaving behind few clues for explorers.

As diving technology has advanced, retrieving valuable items from shipwrecks has become easier. At first, recovering only treasure and cannons was considered worth the risk involved. Later, it became possible to raise the wrecks by patching up holes and pumping in air.

The development of deep-ocean exploration systems was encouraged by the need to find missing submarines and nuclear weapons during the Cold War (1946–1990). It has resulted in spectacular finds, including Dr. Bob Ballard's discovery of the *Titanic* and *Bismarck*.

THE CREW WORKS IN A TITANIUM SPHERE WITH THICK WINDOWS. WATER PRESSURE AT 9,840 FEET (3,000 M) IS 300 TIMES GREATER THAN AIR PRESSURE AT SEA LEVEL.

THE SUBMERSIBLE'S PROPELLER IS PROTECTED BY A LIGHT SCREEN SO THAT PIECES OF RIGGING, WIRE, OR ROPE WILL NOT TRAP THE VESSEL ON THE SEAFLOOR.

A REMOTE MANIPULATOR ARM LIFTS ITEMS FROM THE OCEAN FLOOR. SOME PIECES MAY BE BROUGHT TO THE SURFACE FOR CLOSER EXAMINATION.

Wreck hunting
Finding deep wrecks is not easy because the ocean is so big. First, side-scan sonar and cameras mounted on sleds survey the area where the wreck might be. When the wreck is found, TV cameras attached to remote-operated vehicles (ROVs) begin a detailed exploration of the shipwreck. A submersible like *Alvin* may be used so the explorers can examine the wreck close up.

Viewing the remains
An ROV camera travels inside the wreck to bring back images of familiar objects.

What a side-scan sees
A side-scan sonar gives a one-color image of shadows. Computers help improve the picture quality, but recognizing what the image shows still requires skill and experience.

IT MAY TAKE A SURVEY SHIP WEEKS OF SEARCHING TO FIND THE WRECK.

A CURIOUS WHALE IS ATTRACTED BY SONAR SOUNDS.

THE SIDE-SCAN SONAR GENERATES FAN-SHAPED BEAMS OF SOUND ENERGY, WHICH BOUNCE OFF HARD SURFACES THAT REFLECT WELL.

A CAMERA SLED IS TOWED NEAR THE SEAFLOOR TO TAKE PICTURES OF THE WRECK.

The first images

The bow, or front, of the wreck in this photo is surrounded by the darkness of the deep ocean. Deep-sea wrecks may be draped with a rust-like crust that is produced by iron-eating bacteria.

ALVIN SENDS A SMALL ROV THROUGH A HOLE IN THE WRECK TO TAKE PICTURES OF ITS INTERIOR.

Looking for ancient wrecks

In the warm, clear waters of the Mediterranean, marine archaeologists hunt for the wrecks of ancient Greek, Roman, and Persian ships. The wooden parts will have been eaten away unless they were well-buried, but metal remains can be found by a submersible metal detector.

A diver photographs the cargo of a Roman shipwreck. The diver uses a survey grid to accurately record the position of items.

A cannon is raised using lifting bags that were filled with air on the ocean floor. The diver releases air pressure to control the speed of the climb. Larger bags can raise aircraft, ships, and submarines.

Ocean Life

The oceans teem with a wide variety of life, from tiny bacteria to huge whales. Scientists now believe life on Earth first began in the oceans.

Living things exist throughout the oceans, even in icy, polar waters and the deepest, darkest trenches of the ocean floor. At the surface, tiny floating plants called phytoplankton use the Sun's energy to make food. Sea creatures graze on the plankton and are then eaten by larger hunters and scavengers. Worms, bacteria, and other creatures live in very deep water and the thick mud of the ocean floor. At these depths, there is no light for plants to grow, so deep-sea creatures feed on material that has sunk down from above.

One very unusual group of creatures on the ocean floor feeds on chemicals rather than animal or plant matter. They live near hot-water springs that are full of strong chemicals.

Something for everyone

In the ocean, every possible niche, or living environment, is inhabited by one or more life-forms. Researchers constantly discover new animals as they learn more about the oceans. Scientists were amazed to discover that life could exist around deep-sea hot-water vents. Water gushes up from these cracks at temperatures as high as 752° Fahrenheit (400° Celsius) and carries a dissolved mixture of strong chemicals. Unlike other animals, the creatures near these volcanic vents get energy from eating bacteria. The chemicals the bacteria absorb are changed into energy. Most other organisms get energy from the Sun because plants use sunlight to make food energy, and animals eat plants or plant-eaters.

DEEP-SEA CRABS AND FISH THRIVE NEAR A HOT WATER VENT.

IN WARM, SUNLIT WATERS, PLANTS AND ANIMALS THRIVE.

MOST DRIFTING PLANKTON IS MADE UP OF PHYTOPLANKTON (TINY PLANTS) AND ZOO-PLANKTON (TINY ANIMALS), INCLUDING LARVAE, WHICH ARE THE YOUNG FORMS OF THE ZOOPLANKTON.

USING ITS LONG, STINGING TENTACLES, THE PORTUGUESE MAN-OF-WAR CATCHES PREY.

THE MESOPELAGIC (TWILIGHT) ZONE, FROM 650 TO 3,280 FEET (200 TO 1,000 M), IS HOME TO MANY FISH, SUCH AS THESE HATCHET FISH.

FEW ANIMALS LIVE IN THE DARK, COLD BATHYPELAGIC ZONE, FROM 3,280 TO 9,840 FEET (1,000 TO 3,000 M) DOWN.

TRIPOD FISH AND SEA CUCUMBERS

MINERALS FROM HOT-WATER VENTS FORM CHIMNEYS AROUND THE VENTS.

GIANT TUBE WORMS GROW UP TO 10 FEET (3 M) LONG.

SUNLIGHT PROVIDES THE ENERGY THAT BEGINS THE FOOD CHAIN.

SMALL FISH EAT PLANKTON.

Food chains

In the open ocean, phytoplankton are eaten by zooplankton, which are then eaten by small fish.

ALL THE OCEAN'S PLANTS AND MANY OF ITS ANIMALS LIVE IN THE EPIPELAGIC (SUNLIT) ZONE, DOWN TO 650 FEET (200 M).

The small fish are eaten by larger fish and squid, which are eaten by sharks and toothed whales (*see left*). This is called a food chain. Each group of animals is an important link in the chain and serves as food for another group of animals.

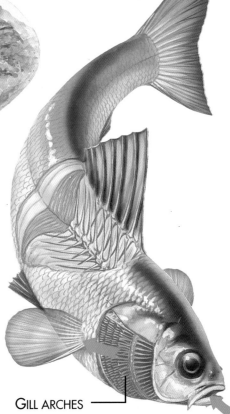

SQUID EAT SMALL FISH.

SPERM WHALES EAT SQUID.

SHARKS HAVE EXISTED FOR MILLIONS OF YEARS.

OCTOPUSES ARE INTELLIGENT CREATURES FOUND IN BOTH DEEP AND SHALLOW WATERS.

A BRITTLE STAR IS ABLE TO LIVE AT GREAT DEPTHS.

GULPER EELS CAN DISLOCATE THEIR JAWS TO SWALLOW LARGE PREY.

ANGLER FISH ATTRACT PREY WITH A LIGHT-EMITTING "ROD" ABOVE THEIR HEAD.

THE ABYSSAL ZONE, FROM 9,840 FEET (3,000 M) TO THE SEA BOTTOM, IS DARK AND FRIGID.

GILL ARCHES ABSORB OXYGEN.

How fish breathe

Fish do not have lungs. They breathe with organs called gills, which can extract the oxygen dissolved in seawater. The fish gulps water into its mouth, and then pushes it out between its gill arches, which are lined with blood-filled cells. Here, oxygen passes from the seawater into the fish's blood, and waste gases flow out of the fish back into the seawater. Some of the gas that the fish extracts from the water inflates a swim bladder, which helps keep the fish from sinking.

Coastal Life

Animals and plants that live on the coast must have the ability to adapt to periods in and out of the water as the tides change the sea level. Some seaweeds produce slime to help stop them from drying out during low tide. Many animals burrow into the wet sand, hide under seaweed, or close up their shells while the tide is low. Coastal plants and animals in exposed places need to be strong enough to survive the crashing waves and to adapt to changes in the saltiness of the water when it rains.

A much greater variety of animals and plants lives in rock pools because there they will not dry out when the tide goes down. But they still have to cope with freshwater when it rains as well as large changes in temperature when the pool warms up in the sunlight or cools down in cold or dark.

Coastal life zones
The splash zone lies above high tide but is regularly sprayed with saltwater. It is a hard place to live, and few species are seen here. Snails and yellow, orange, and black lichens are typical inhabitants.

The intertidal zone, between high and low tide, is home to creatures such as barnacles, limpets, mussels, sea anemones, and crabs. Plants include brown, green, and red seaweeds.

Below low-tide level live many more kinds of plants and animals. In cold waters, great forests of large brown seaweeds, called kelp, live on rocks. Kelp forests shelter delicate red seaweeds, fish, and many other animals. In warm waters, coral reefs thrive.

SEAWEEDS SECURELY ATTACH THEMSELVES TO ROCKS.

SAND, GRAVEL, MUD, AND ROCK FORM THE SEABED.

Burrowing on the beach
Many animals skillfully burrow in the sand. With her hind flippers, the female loggerhead turtle digs a hole in which to lay her eggs (1). Razor clams (2) have long shells with a powerful "foot" at the bottom to help the clams move up or down.

The sand gaper (3) has an oval shell and feeds through two tubes that stretch up to the surface. Sea potatoes (4) are burrowing sea urchins. The sea mouse (5) is a worm covered with fine hairs. Lugworms (6) swallow sand to feed, then pass out what is left over as worm casts.

TO RECEIVE SUNLIGHT, THE LEAVES OF THIS GIANT KELP STRETCH UP TOWARD THE SURFACE WATERS.

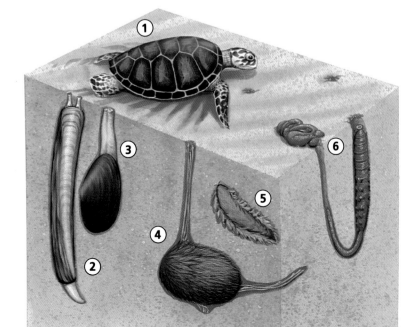

SEAWEEDS CLING FIRMLY TO ROCKS SO THAT THEY ARE NOT SWEPT OUT TO SEA.

SEABIRDS OFTEN NEST ON CLIFFS NEAR THEIR FOOD SUPPLY.

LICHENS ARE FORMED BY A FUNGUS AND A KIND OF ALGAE LIVING TOGETHER.

SEA SLATERS FEED ON SEAWEED AND DEAD ANIMALS.

PERIWINKLES CAN BE ROLLED BY WAVES WITHOUT BEING DAMAGED.

Limpets

When the tide goes out, limpets clamp their shells firmly to rocks, which stops their bodies from drying out. A suckerlike foot allows them to crawl along.

A CROSS SECTION OF A LIMPET REVEALS ITS STOMACH AND OTHER ORGANS.

AIR-FILLED SACS KEEP SOME BROWN SEAWEEDS AFLOAT.

A CRAB'S SOFTER UNDERBODY IS PROTECTED BY THE HARD SHELL ON ITS BACK.

Crabs

Crabs of several types live on the coast. Their shells protect them well. Crabs use their pincers to crush the shells of their prey.

THE SEA URCHIN'S GUT LIES IN THE CENTER OF ITS BODY, ABOVE FIVE SHARP TEETH.

Sea urchins and starfish

Sea urchins have a protective outer covering of spines and a shell made of layers of interlocking plates. The spines and suckerlike feet allow urchins to move around on the seabed and coast. Five teeth under its body scrape food off the rocks.

Starfish are in the same family as sea urchins. Under the arms of a starfish are rows of tubelike feet used for moving and feeding.

Mangroves

Mangrove trees are unusual because they can live in salty seawater. The mass of tangled roots in a mangrove swamp collects mud and provides homes for young fish, the saltwater crocodile, and sea snakes. The mud skipper (*above*) is a small fish that can walk on its front fins and climb up the mangrove roots. It feeds on small animals in the mud at low tide.

Seabirds

Seabirds live near all the world's oceans, from the freezing waters of the Antarctic to the warmth of tropical waters. Some, such as the albatross and storm petrel, spend most of their lives at sea, returning to the land only once a year to breed and to shed old feathers, or molt.

Seabirds eat fish, squid, or plankton, and they may travel great distances to find this food. To stay warm in cold seawater, most birds have a layer of fat under their skin, and they have feathers that are oiled to keep them waterproof. Unlike other seabirds, the cormorant rests out of the water with its wings outstretched to dry in the Sun.

Seabirds have few natural enemies, but many are killed accidentally by humans. Pollution poisons some, while other seabirds get tangled in fishing nets.

The brown pelican
Brown pelicans live in coastal areas of the United States. On the underside of their beaks, they have large, baggy pouches that they use to catch many small fish.

The pelican flies around looking for fish swimming near the water's surface. When it spots a shoal of fish, the bird dives gracefully into the water and surprises the fish. The pelican swims around, scooping the fish into its beak's pouch; then it returns to the water's surface to swallow them.

THE BROWN PELICAN FLIES SLIGHTLY ABOVE THE WATER'S SURFACE LOOKING FOR FISH.

AS IT SPOTS A GROUP OF FISH CLOSE TO THE SURFACE, THE PELICAN DIVES INTO THE SEA, FOLDING ITS WINGS.

THE STORM PETREL HOVERS JUST ABOVE THE SURFACE.

ONCE IN THE WATER, THE PELICAN SCOOPS UP AS MANY FISH AS POSSIBLE.

THE AUK USES ITS STUMPY WINGS TO "FLY" UNDERWATER.

FISH SLIDE HEAD FIRST DOWN THE PELICAN'S GULLET.

THE FISH THEN TRAVEL TOWARD THE STOMACH.

Feeding

Seabirds catch food in many different ways. At night, skimmers fly low over the surface and use the tips of their beaks to scoop up small fish and shrimps. The storm petrel hovers over the sea surface, picking up individual fish. The auk, from the family that includes the puffin and razorbill, dives under the sea to chase fish using its powerful, stumpy wings and webbed feet. The albatross glides effortlessly, landing occasionally to catch fish or squid on the surface.

Puffin nest
Puffins live in noisy groups on isolated islands away from land predators, such as rats and foxes. They nest inside tunnels, among rocks, or in abandoned burrows. Puffins use their sharp claws and feet to dig their own burrows.

ALBATROSSES CATCH FISH WHILE FLOATING ON THE SURFACE.

THE BLUE-FOOTED BOOBY HAS A SHALLOW DIVING ANGLE.

SKIMMERS FLY FROM DUSK TO DAWN, SCOOPING UP FOOD FROM THE WATER'S SURFACE.

Kittiwake gull nest
Kittiwake gulls attach their cup-shaped nests to narrow cliff-side ledges by using their droppings as a kind of glue.

THE CORMORANT HAS A STEEP, STREAMLINED DIVE AND USES ITS FEET TO PUSH ITSELF THROUGH THE WATER.

PENGUINS CATCH FISH AND SQUID BY SWIMMING QUICKLY UNDERWATER.

FISH, SQUID, AND PLANKTON ARE FOOD FOR SEABIRDS.

Guillemot nest
Guillemots nest on rock ledges that have sheer drops to the sea below. They lay pointed eggs that are less likely to fall off if they are accidentally knocked.

Coral Reefs

Coral looks and feels like rock, but it is made by tiny animals related to jellyfish and sea anemones. These animals, called polyps, build a stony, cup-shaped skeleton around themselves. As the polyps multiply, new polyps grow on the skeletons of dead polyps. Thousands of these polyps together form a clump of coral. Corals are highly sensitive to pollution and to rapid changes in sea level and temperature. They mainly grow in shallow, tropical waters.

Coral reefs form walls along coastlines, often creating a calm, shallow lagoon inside the coral walls. Life flourishes in these sheltered, food-rich lagoons. Thousands of brightly colored fish make use of the coral reef in different ways; some graze, while others hide from predators hunting them.

YOUNG ANGELFISH

BUTTERFLY FISH RECOGNIZE EACH OTHER BY THEIR MARKINGS.

SEA CUCUMBERS ARE IN THE SAME ANIMAL GROUP AS STARFISH AND SEA URCHINS.

GIANT CLAMS GROW SLOWLY AND MAY LIVE FOR ONE HUNDRED YEARS.

DELICATE SEA FANS LIVE IN DEEPER WATER AWAY FROM DAMAGING WAVES.

CLOWN FISH ARE ABLE TO HIDE IN ANEMONES, WHICH STING OTHER FISH.

A GROUPER LETS A CLEANER WRASSE REMOVE PARASITES LIVING IN ITS MOUTH.

THE CROWN OF THORNS STARFISH ATTACKS CORAL.

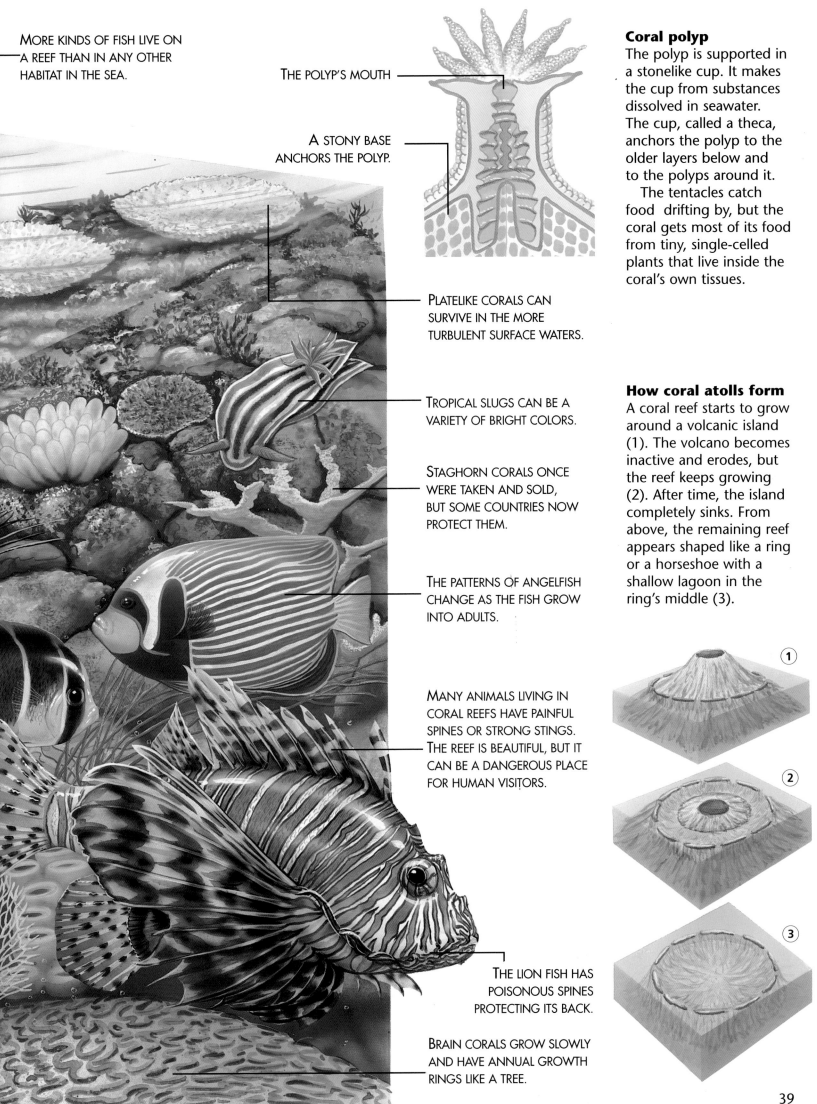

MORE KINDS OF FISH LIVE ON A REEF THAN IN ANY OTHER HABITAT IN THE SEA.

THE POLYP'S MOUTH

A STONY BASE ANCHORS THE POLYP.

PLATELIKE CORALS CAN SURVIVE IN THE MORE TURBULENT SURFACE WATERS.

TROPICAL SLUGS CAN BE A VARIETY OF BRIGHT COLORS.

STAGHORN CORALS ONCE WERE TAKEN AND SOLD, BUT SOME COUNTRIES NOW PROTECT THEM.

THE PATTERNS OF ANGELFISH CHANGE AS THE FISH GROW INTO ADULTS.

MANY ANIMALS LIVING IN CORAL REEFS HAVE PAINFUL SPINES OR STRONG STINGS. THE REEF IS BEAUTIFUL, BUT IT CAN BE A DANGEROUS PLACE FOR HUMAN VISITORS.

THE LION FISH HAS POISONOUS SPINES PROTECTING ITS BACK.

BRAIN CORALS GROW SLOWLY AND HAVE ANNUAL GROWTH RINGS LIKE A TREE.

Coral polyp

The polyp is supported in a stonelike cup. It makes the cup from substances dissolved in seawater. The cup, called a theca, anchors the polyp to the older layers below and to the polyps around it.

The tentacles catch food drifting by, but the coral gets most of its food from tiny, single-celled plants that live inside the coral's own tissues.

How coral atolls form

A coral reef starts to grow around a volcanic island (1). The volcano becomes inactive and erodes, but the reef keeps growing (2). After time, the island completely sinks. From above, the remaining reef appears shaped like a ring or a horseshoe with a shallow lagoon in the ring's middle (3).

1
2
3

Ocean Pollution

Almost all rivers and drainage systems eventually flow into the ocean, carrying waste products from human activities out to sea. The ocean has become like an enormous sink, holding chemicals, sewage, and rubbish from wars, accidents, and deliberate dumping. Of course, the ocean is very large, and not all pollutants cause major problems. Also, some kinds of bacteria will eat up oil spills or digest steel. Over many years, the ocean can clean itself very well. But where pollutants are concentrated, they can do a great deal of damage. Coastal waters beside large cities, intensively farmed land, or heavy industries can become so polluted that natural cleaning systems cannot cope. The result can be death for marine life, ugly pollution along coastlines, and damaged health for the human population.

Today, scientists are doing research to find out how much waste can safely be allowed into the oceans. Many countries are trying to control pollution.

Poisonous waters

There are so many sources of pollution that it is difficult to know exactly what is being poured into the sea. Chemicals that are harmless on their own blend with others and produce dangerous mixtures that can have unexpected effects. Nutrients in sewage and fertilizers can make poisonous plankton grow at an alarming rate, causing plankton blooms, or red tides.

HOUSING DEVELOPMENTS NEAR THE COAST INCREASE LOCAL POLLUTION LEVELS.

SEWERS CAN LEAK SEWAGE INTO GROUNDWATER AND SPOIL WATER SUPPLIES.

SOME OF THE CHEMICALS SPRAYED ON CROPS WASH INTO RIVERS AND OCEANS.

POISONOUS PLANKTON THRIVES IN SOME POLLUTED SEAS AND COLORS THE WATER.

SEWAGE SLUDGE DUMPED FROM A SHIP IS POISONOUS TO MARINE LIFE.

MINING WASTE DUMPED INTO THE WATER CAN SMOTHER THE SEAFLOOR, KILL MARINE LIFE, AND POISON THE WATER.

Fertilizer damage

Farmers use large quantities of artificial fertilizer, so they can grow as many crops as possible. Some of the fertilizer gets washed into rivers by rainfall. Rivers carry it into coastal waters. The fertilizer makes local marine plants grow at a greater rate. The fast-growing plants can crowd the places where other animals and plants would normally live. When the plants start to rot, they begin to smell and attract many insects.

OLD WATERWAYS THAT ARE
NO LONGER USED CAN
BECOME HEAVILY POLLUTED,
ESPECIALLY WHERE THE
WATER FLOWS SLOWLY.

THE WIND MAY BLOW
DIRTY FACTORY SMOKE
OUT TO SEA.

HEAVY PARTICLES FROM
FACTORY SMOKE EITHER FALL,
OR THE WIND AND RAIN
CARRY THEM TO THE OCEAN.

DANGEROUS CHEMICALS
FROM LANDFILLS LEAK INTO
THE WATER SUPPLY OVER
MANY YEARS.

SOME MICROSCOPIC
PLANKTON ARE VERY
POISONOUS AND CAN
CONTAMINATE THE
SEAFOOD WE EAT.

OBJECTS ON
THE SEAFLOOR
CAN BECOME BURIED
UNDER A LAYER OF SILT.

SOME SHIPS DISCHARGE
BALLAST WATER, LEAKING
WASTES AND MARINE LIFE
FROM OTHER WATERS.

A SHIPWRECK CAN CAUSE
POLLUTION, BUT IT MAY
ALSO PROVIDE SHELTER FOR
YOUNG FISH, PROTECTING
THEM FROM FISHING NETS.

Dumping at sea
Coastal seas have been
used as a dumping
ground for sewage (1),
old ships (2), chemical
wastes (3), and even
discarded weapons. Oil
rigs (4) may be dumped
at the end of their
working lives, too. Oil
is washed from ships
or accidentally leaks
out when oil tankers
run aground. Oil slicks (5)
and the chemicals used to
clean them up can kill sea
life. Even the special paint
used on boats, if it spills
(6), can harm sea life.

41

Mining the Sea

Vast reserves of oil, gas, and coal, as well as valuable minerals and metals, lie under the ocean floor. The seafloor also has valuable reserves of sand and gravel, which can be used in building roads and for general construction. Occasionally, the sand and gravel contain diamonds or other precious substances.

When plentiful reserves of a natural resource, such as coal, occur on land, it is unnecessary and too expensive to mine that resource from beneath the sea. However, since oil and gas are so valuable, some companies believe that the difficulty and cost of drilling exploration wells, building offshore platforms, and sending oil and gas to the shore are worthwhile.

In the future, when raw materials run out on land, other products will be mined from the sea as well.

A FLARE STACK BURNS OFF EXCESS GAS.

Oil platform
The superstructure is built with several modules, or parts, which are lifted onto the jacket, or frame, by cranes. There are modules for power, engineering, pump rooms, living areas, dining, medical services, and entertainment.

GAS-TURBINE EXHAUSTS

THE STEEL JACKET, OR FRAMEWORK, IS REGULARLY MAINTAINED BY DIVERS AND UNDERWATER ROBOTS.

A PIPE FROM THIS DERRICK CARRIES OIL AND GAS TO THE SURFACE.

ORGANIC MATERIAL RAINS ONTO THE SEABED.

INCREASING PRESSURE AND TEMPERATURE GRADUALLY CAUSE HYDROCARBONS TO FORM.

Formation of oil and gas
Organic matter, such as plankton, drifts to the seabed and gets buried (*right, top*). Over time, the layers of decomposing matter deepen, and their temperature and pressure increase. Chemical reactions and bacteria slowly change the organic matter into hydrocarbons, such as oil and gas (*right, middle*). Along geological faults, the oil and gas may get trapped behind layers of rock (*right, bottom*).

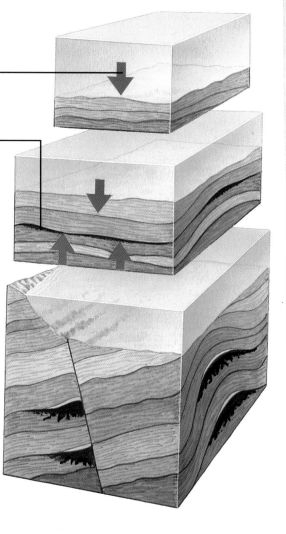

A DERRICK IS THE TOWER OVER A DRILL.

CRANE TO UNLOAD SUPPLY SHIPS

HELICOPTERS TRANSFER CREWS TO AND FROM THE PLATFORMS.

HELIPAD FOR HELICOPTER LANDINGS

LIFEBOATS ARE DESIGNED FOR ESCAPE THROUGH BURNING SEAS.

PIPELINES FLOW TO THE SHORE AND NEARBY WELLS.

THE PLATFORM IS ANCHORED IN PLACE WITH LONG STEEL PINS.

THE DRILL PENETRATES THE OIL DEPOSIT.

SOME OIL IS TRAPPED BEHIND DENSE ROCKS.

Oil-production platform

The basic oil-production platform consists of a steel-jacket framework (1) extending from the seafloor up to a height above the highest possible waves. The superstructure built on this (2) carries all of the equipment needed to safely drill holes in the seabed, suck oil out of the deposit, carefully control the rate of flow, and pump it either along a pipeline to a shore base (3) or load it directly onto oil tankers. The platform is powered by gas turbines (4), which provide power and pressurize the oil well to make the oil rise faster.

Gas comes up with the oil. Some is injected back into the underground deposit; some is used to fuel the turbines, and, if there is enough, it is separated and sent to shore. Any excess is burned off at the end of long booms, or arms (5).

Platform types

Besides the steel-jacket rig, there are many different platforms: a floating platform held by anchors (*above, left*) is used in deep water or for smaller oil fields; a very large concrete platform (*above, center*) is able to withstand severe weather and has storage tanks built into the base; and a seafloor well head (*above, right*) is installed by a drilling ship and then left in deep waters to pump oil to shore automatically.

Ocean Power

The sea creates huge amounts of energy that people can use to generate electricity without causing pollution or releasing harmful gases that change the climate. Power from the sea will never run out. So why has it taken so long to develop sea power? People believed it would be too expensive to build and set up the necessary equipment. Large, complex machines need to be built, then towed out to rough waters, and moored, or anchored, into position. The machines would have to work for many years before the sale of power would pay for building and installing them, and even longer before any profit was made. Today, pollution is taken more seriously, and people are beginning to use alternative energy forms, such as sea power.

Thermal power

Ocean Thermal Energy Conversion (OTEC) uses the difference in temperature between warm surface water and deep cold water to evaporate liquid ammonia and spin a turbine electrical generator. OTEC works best in the tropics, where the cold water can be piped to nearby islands after use.

The picture (*right*) and diagram (*below, right*) show how the system works. Heat transferred from warm surface water boils liquid ammonia to make it into a vapor (1). The ammonia vapor spins a turbine to make electricity (2). Very cold water is drawn up from deep in the ocean (3) and condenses the ammonia back into liquid (4). The ammonia travels back to the tank (5) to be used over and over again.

CROSS SECTION OF A THERMAL POWER PLANT

THE TOP OF THE BARRAGE IS USED AS A ROAD BRIDGE.

A GENERATOR USES THE WATER'S ENERGY TO MAKE ELECTRICITY.

A TURBINE CAPTURES THE ENERGY OF THE FLOWING WATER.

WARM SURFACE WATER MORE THAN 77° FAHRENHEIT (25° C) BOILS AMMONIA.

LIQUID AMMONIA RETURNS TO THE TANK FOR REUSE MANY TIMES.

Tidal power barrage

People first used sea power by building dams across estuaries. At high tide, the estuary would fill up. At low tide, the water was released, passing across a waterwheel attached to a mill for grinding grain. In today's design, called a tidal power barrage, the water spins a turbine to make electricity.

COLD WATER BELOW 41° FAHRENHEIT (5° C) IS PIPED FROM MORE THAN 1,641 FEET (500 M) DEEP.

WAVES ENTERING A BAY ARE FUNNELED TOWARD A CLIFF.

A SURGE GENERATOR OPERATES WITHIN A CLIFF.

FLOATING POWER STATIONS TRANSMIT ELECTRICITY BACK TO SHORE.

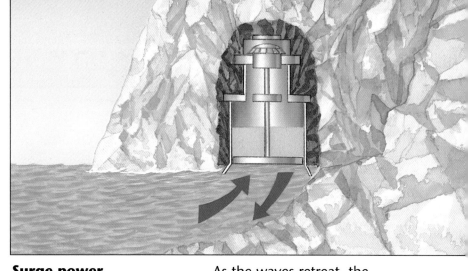

Surge power

A few power plants use power generated from a piston's up-and-down movement. Waves entering a bay force the piston upward. As the waves retreat, the piston falls back into position, ready for the next wave. A surge generator is able to make power from the force of every wave.

A ROW OF HOLLOW FLOATS CALLED SALTER'S DUCKS *(see below)* EXTRACTS POWER FROM PASSING WAVES.

②

④

⑤

③

COLD WATER CONDENSES THE AMMONIA BACK INTO LIQUID.

AFTER USE, THE WARM WATER IS RETURNED TO THE OCEAN.

AFTERWARD, THE COLD WATER CAN BE PIPED TO NEARBY ISLANDS FOR FARMERS TO USE.

WAVE FORCES THE SALTER DUCK'S SHELL UPWARD.

THE ROCKING MOTION IS USED TO GENERATE ELECTRICITY.

Wave power

Offshore, the constant rise and fall of the sea can be harnessed by devices such as Salter's Nodding Ducks. These are hollow concrete floats, each one about 108 feet (33 m) long and 66 feet (20 m) across. Incoming waves push the duck up, transferring the force to a system of electricity generators. Fifty or more ducks connected together form a very efficient generation system.

Glossary

abyssal plain: the deep, dark ocean floor.

ballast: large tanks that are filled with water to lower a vessel, or with air to raise a vessel.

buoy: a floating marker in the ocean.

continental shelf: a continent's sloping, lower part that is covered by seawater near the coast.

crust: the thin, outer layer of Earth.

current: the directional movement of water.

equator: an imaginary line around Earth's middle at an equal distance from both poles.

erosion: wearing away due to water, wind, or ice.

food chain: a natural system where animals and plants feed on smaller organisms in the chain.

gale: a very strong wind or storm.

gill: a fish organ that absorbs oxygen from water.

glacier: a huge ice sheet found in polar regions.

groin: a jetty, or wall, built to preserve a beach from water erosion.

icebreaker: a ship specially designed to break up and make paths through ice sheets.

lagoon: a shallow pool of seawater separated from the sea by a narrow strip of land.

longshore drift: the zigzag pattern caused by waves moving sand and fragments along coastlines.

mantle: the rocky, middle layer of Earth.

neoprene: a synthetic rubber used in diving suits.

oceanographer: a scientist who studies the oceans and the animals and plants that live in them.

ooze: a thick layer of fine-grained sediment, or mud.

orbit (n): the path an object follows as it circles a larger object in space.

neap tide: a small high tide occurring when the gravitational pulls of the Moon and Sun do not line up.

phytoplankton: microscopic plants that live in ocean waters.

plate: a huge, slowly moving piece of Earth's crust and upper mantle.

predator: an animal that hunts and eats animals.

prey: animals that are eaten by other animals.

propeller: a set of rotating blades that provides the force needed to move a vehicle through water.

rudder: a thin, hinged wood or metal plate used for steering ships. Rudders are attached to the back.

satellite: a spacecraft that orbits Earth. Satellites record information and send it back to Earth.

scavengers: organisms that feed on dead things and clean up waste matter.

scuba: **S**elf-**C**ontained **U**nderwater **B**reathing **A**pparatus. Scuba equipment allows people to breathe while they are diving underwater.

sea level: the average level of the ocean's surface.

sediment: layers of mud, particles, clay, and sand.

sonar: **So**und **Na**vigation **R**anging. Sonar instruments send sound waves through water and record information when the sound waves bounce back off of solid objects, like the seabed.

spring tide: very high tide occurring when the gravity of the Sun and Moon pull together in line.

stabilizer: the finlike arms extending from a ship's body to reduce roll and help keep it upright.

subduction zone: where two of Earth's plates meet and rock is drawn down to melt below the crust.

submersible: a small vehicle for fairly short, deep dives, often equipped with cameras, windows, and special instruments used by scientists.

tidal range: the difference between the usual high-water and low-water levels.

tide: the periodic rising and falling, due to the Moon's gravity, of the water level in the oceans.

volcanic vent: a crack through which hot water gushes from under the deep-sea floor. The water contains a dissolved mixture of strong chemicals.

zooplankton: microscopic animals that live and float in the ocean waters.

More Books to Read

Amazing Sea Creatures. Extraordinary Animals (series). Andrew Brown (Crabtree)

Beneath the Oceans. Worldwise (series). Penny Clarke (Franklin Watts)

Beneath the Waves: Exploring the Hidden World of the Kelp Forest. Norbert Wu (Chronicle Books)

The Coral Reef. The Deep Blue Planet (series). Renato Massa (Raintree Steck-Vaughn)

Creeps from the Deep. Leighton R. Taylor (Chronicle Books)

Discovering Marine Mammals. Nancy Field and Sally Machlis (Dog Eared)

Oceans and Seas. Alex Voglino and Renato Massa (Raintree Steck-Vaughn)

Oceans and Seas. Habitats (series). Ewan McLeish (Thomson Learning)

The Pacific Ocean. Seas and Oceans (series). David Lambert (Raintree Steck-Vaughn)

Polar Seas. Seas and Oceans (series). Malcolm Penny (Raintree Steck-Vaughn)

The Red Sea and the Arabian Gulf. Seas and Oceans (series). Julia Waterlow (Raintree Steck-Vaughn)

Seas & Oceans. Take Five Geography (series). Jane Parker and Steve Parker (Franklin Watts)

Videos

Henry's Amazing Animals: Underwater Animals. (Dorling Kindersley)

In the Company of Whales. (Discovery Communication)

In the Wild — Dolphins With Robin Williams. (PBS Home Video)

National Geographic's Amazing Planet: Shark-a-Thon. (National Geographic Kids Video)

National Geographic's Ocean Drifters. (National Geographic)

Web Sites

Deep Sea Machines (Nova Online)
www.pbs.org/wgbh/nova/abyss/frontier/deepsea.html

Diving: Human Contact with the Underwater World
library.thinkquest.org/28170/3.html

EPA Office of Wetlands, Oceans, and Watersheds
www.epa.gov/OWOW/index.html

The Evergreen Project
http://mbgnet.mobot.org/index2.htm

The Nature of Water
www.ec.gc.ca/water/en/nature/e_nature.htm

Oceans Alive
www.abc.net.au/oceans/alive.htm

Underwater Caves of El Jacinto Pat
www.cavedive.com/

U.S. Coast Guard International Ice Patrol
www. uscg.mil/lantera/iip/home.html
(Choose *Other Links*)

Some web sites stay current longer than others. For further web sites, use your search engines to locate the following topics: *Jacques Cousteau, currents, oceanography, plankton, scuba, submarines,* and *Titanic.*

Index